D0845646

THE SCIENCE OF
HUMAN FLIGHT

Jordan Johnson

Cavendish
Square

New York

SOMERSET CO. LIBRARY
BRIDGEWATER, NJ 08807

Published in 2019 by Cavendish Square Publishing, LLC
243 5th Avenue, Suite 136, New York, NY 10016

Copyright © 2019 by Cavendish Square Publishing, LLC

First Edition

No part of this publication may be reproduced, stored in a retrieval system, or transmitted in any form or by any means—electronic, mechanical, photocopying, recording, or otherwise—without the prior permission of the copyright owner. Request for permission should be addressed to Permissions, Cavendish Square Publishing, 243 5th Avenue, Suite 136, New York, NY 10016. Tel (877) 980-4450; fax (877) 980-4454.

Website: cavendishsq.com

This publication represents the opinions and views of the author based on his or her personal experience, knowledge, and research. The information in this book serves as a general guide only. The author and publisher have used their best efforts in preparing this book and disclaim liability rising directly or indirectly from the use and application of this book.

All websites were available and accurate when this book was sent to press.

Library of Congress Cataloging-in-Publication Data

Names: Johnson, Jordan (Children's author), author.
Title: The science of human flight / Jordan Johnson.
Description: First edition. | New York : Cavendish Square, 2019. | Series: The science of superpowers | Audience: Grades 3-6. | Includes index.
Identifiers: LCCN 2017048033| ISBN 9781502637871 (library bound) | ISBN 9781502637888 (pbk.) | 9781502637895 (ebook)
Subjects: LCSH: Flight--Juvenile literature. | Aerodynamics--Juvenile literature. | Aeronautics--Juvenile literature. | CYAC: Flight. | Aerodynamics. | Aeronautics.
Classification: LCC TL547 .J54 2019 | DDC 629.1309--dc23
LC record available at https://lccn.loc.gov/2017048033

Editorial Director: David McNamara
Editor: Kristen Susienka
Copy Editor: Rebecca Rohan
Associate Art Director: Amy Greenan
Designer: Joe Parenteau
Production Coordinator: Karol Szymczuk
Photo Research: J8 Media

The photographs in this book are used by permission and through the courtesy of: Cover Erik Isakson/Blend Images/ Getty Images, Background Keith Pomakis/Wikimedia Commons/File:Cumulus Clouds Over Jamaica.jpg/BY SA-2.5; p. 4 Joggiebotma/iStock/Thinkstock; p. 7 Banet/Shutterstock.com; p. 9 W.G. Collingwood/Wikimedia Commons/ File:Odin rides to Hel.jpg/CCO; p. 11 Artpritsadee/Shutterstock.com; p. 12 Hulton Archive/Getty Images; p. 14 Matthias Clamer/Stone/Getty Images; p. 16 Carlos Clarivan/Science Source˙ p. 17 Mike Watson Images/Moodboard/ Thinkstock; p. 18 Maxisport/Shutterstock.com; p. 22 Jonathan Murrish/EyeEm/Getty Images; p. 24 Jeffrey Ong Guo Xiong/Shutterstock.com; p. 26 ©iStockphoto.com/CraigRJD; p. 28 Jr Nicholas/Science Source/Getty Images; p. 29 Ondrej Prosicky/Shutterstock.com; p. 31 Anchorage Daily News/Tribune News Service/Getty Images; p. 33 Nlitement/ Wikimedia Commons/ File:Helicopter leaves.jpg/BY SA-3.0; p. 34 Corbis Historical/Getty Images; p. 36 ©iStockphoto. com/gk-6mt; p. 38 Robyn Beck/AFP/Getty Images; p. 39 Simon Holdcroft/Alamy Stock Photo; p. 42 Dave Turner/ Shutterstock.com.

Printed in the United States of America

CONTENTS

CHAPTER 1

ORIGIN STORIES

For countless years, people have told stories about amazing humans accomplishing the seemingly impossible. Usually, these "superhumans" can do tasks better than normal people. Other times, they can do things average people can't do at all, such as fly.

Many superheroes in today's stories can fly. Some have wings to move them through

Opposite: Skydiving, pictured here, is one of many ways humans can enjoy being off the ground for a while.

the air, while others have magic capes. Some use psychic powers to lift themselves up. A few have special vehicles that help them fly.

Human flight is a fantastic idea, but it's not a new one. People have been telling similar tales of flying legends for hundreds of years.

Some of the most well-known stories of flying come from **myths**. Many ancient cultures around the world told stories of gods, people, and animals that could fly. Gods were often said to fly because of their amazing powers. Any character who could fly was more heroic simply because everyday people couldn't fly on their own. Something that was normally unable to fly could be made mythical very quickly by adding wings.

GREEK MYTHS

Ancient Greece had several stories of characters who could fly. The Greek god Zeus was said to be able to turn into any animal he wished, including flying animals. Hermes, the god of travel, had magic sandals with wings that let him fly and travel very quickly. Greek stories had mythical flying beasts too. Pegasus was a legendary horse with wings. Another mythical creature that could fly was the gryphon. Gryphons were described as having the head and wings of an eagle, but the body and tail of a lion. The idea of a ferocious lion was made more fearsome by the eagle's flight and good eyesight.

This damaged statue of Icarus lies outside the Temple of Concordia in Sicily, Italy.

   Greek myth had stories about everyday humans flying too. Usually, these stories were told to teach a lesson. One such story is that of Icarus and his father, Daedalus. Daedalus was a famous builder. He was tasked with making a maze, called the Labyrinth. The Labyrinth was used to confuse and contain the enemies of Minos, who was the king of the land. When Daedalus helped an enemy of the king escape the Labyrinth, Minos imprisoned both Daedalus and Icarus.

To escape, Daedalus created wings out of wax and feathers. He made one pair for himself and one for his son. Before they flew away, Daedalus warned Icarus of the dangers of using the wings. If Icarus flew too low, the wings would get wet from the ocean, and he'd fall. If he flew too high, the hot sun would melt the wax, and Icarus would fall. The story ends with Icarus flying too close to the sun, then falling into the sea and drowning when his wings melt. The point of the story was to warn against being too lazy or too overconfident.

OTHER MYTHS

Legends of flying humans can also be found in other cultures. Ancient Egyptian and Norse cultures are two examples. Norse mythology has multiple characters who drove flying chariots. Thor, the Norse god of thunder, had a chariot pulled by two flying goats. Freya, a hunting goddess, had a feathery cloak that allowed her

This illustration shows the Norse god Odin riding his eight-legged horse, Sleipnir.

to fly. Odin, the leader of the Norse gods, had an eight-legged horse that could fly, named Sleipnir.

Egyptian myths also had flying characters. Horus was a god of the sun and sky. He had the head of a bird and could fly. Thoth, the god of wisdom, math, and writing, also had the head of a bird. He could change shape into a bird.

IN THE REAL WORLD

Although stories of human flight have been told for thousands of years, humans have been trying to find ways to fly for a long time too. Today, in order to fly, humans mostly rely on **aircraft**. However, some of the earliest attempts at creating flying machines involved imitating birds. One very early flying invention was the rocket. It uses burning fuel in a tube to lift off. Even though they were invented more than a thousand years ago, rockets wouldn't safely carry people until the **space race** in the 1950s.

Other attempts at flight involved using hot air. Hot air balloons use a flame to heat the air inside of the balloon. Air becomes lighter and less dense when it is heated. The hot air mixing with the cool air outside the balloon lifts the balloon and the basket and passengers below. Blimps and other flying balloons, called dirigibles, use a similar idea. The main difference between blimps and dirigibles is that blimps don't have a sturdy skeleton and dirigibles do. Both blimps and dirigibles contain large amounts of hydrogen or helium gas. These gases are lighter than air. They lift up the aircraft.

A group of hot air balloons flies over the landscape. They are all different colors and patterns.

THE WRIGHT BROTHERS

The history of flight was changed forever in the early 1900s. In the late 1800s and early 1900s, brothers Orville and Wilbur Wright started building a flying machine. They tried many designs. Over time, the brothers discovered that certain wing shapes were better at **gliding**. Gliding is like flying but with less ability to stay in the air. All they needed was something to keep pushing the glider while it was in the air. After several attempts, the brothers thought they were ready to try to fly.

In 1903, the Wright brothers

DID YOU KNOW?

The Wright brothers' flyer from 1904 had a top speed of 30 miles per hour (48.2 kilometers per hour), which is slower than most cars today. The fastest aircraft today is the X-15. It can reach top speeds of 4,520 miles per hour (7,274 kmh).

The 1903 Wright flyer, shown below, is mostly made of wood and fabric.

Da Vinci's Helicopter

One of the earliest known attempts at designing a flying machine was made by Leonardo da Vinci. He was a famous artist and engineer who lived in Italy in the 1400s. His design for a flying machine was called the Aerial Screw. It consisted of a small body with a rotating spiral-shaped blade on top. The blade was to spin and "drill" into the air, much like the grooves of a metal screw grab onto a piece of wood when spun. The idea for the Aerial Screw is similar to how modern-day helicopters work.

built and tested a flying machine in Kitty Hawk, North Carolina. Only a few people saw their first successful flight. Many people didn't believe it happened. After many setbacks attempting to do it again, the Wright brothers flew once more in 1904. Using designs and notes from the brothers' research, people from all over the world began building their own similar flying machines. Over time, the machines got faster and could fly farther. The world of aviation was born, and has grown rapidly ever since.

CHAPTER 2

TAKING OFF

Stories and legends about human flight are great, but could it ever happen? Could a human being ever fly on their own? Understanding how flight works is the first step in answering this question.

THE FORCES OF FLIGHT

The science of flight might seem complicated at first. However, it all boils down to four

Opposite: This picture demonstrates what unassisted human flight might look like.

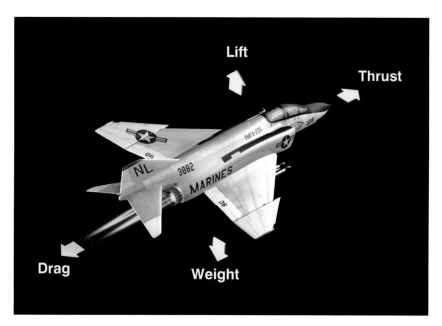

This image illustrates the four forces of flight.

simple **forces**. These forces play a huge role in determining whether something can fly.

The first force is one that all people are familiar with: **gravity**. Gravity is the force that pulls all things on Earth downward. Gravity is the reason for the saying, "What goes up must come down." It is one of the biggest obstacles to flight.

Since gravity is a force that pulls down, flight must have some way to beat it. It requires an opposite force that can push an object upwards. Scientists who study flight call this upward force

lift. In order for something to fly, it has to have more lift than the force of gravity. There are many ways for a flyer or aircraft to gain lift. Helicopters gain lift by using their blades to push air downward. Hot air balloons, blimps, and dirigibles all gain lift by holding large amounts of gas that are less dense than regular air. Planes and other winged aircraft create lift when air passes its specially designed wings.

The next force involved with flight is also familiar to many people. It's called **thrust**, and it's the force of forward movement. People experience the force of thrust almost every day. When people

Jumping can make it seem like people fly through the air. However, it only gets humans off the ground for a few seconds.

US Olympic sprinter Ashley Spencer uses her feet and legs to push her forward as she runs.

walk, their legs push back against the ground and thrust them forward. When people ride in a car or bus, the wheels push against the ground, providing thrust that pushes the car forward. Birds and airplanes gain lift by pushing air backward. Planes do so with their engines.

The last force of flight is **drag**. People feel drag when they run or ride a bike. It's the force of the air pushing on them as they move. It is the force of air resistance on something moving in any direction. The faster anything tries to move, the more drag it has to manage. Most aircraft and flying animals beat the force of drag by having sleek shapes that can cut through the air. They can also use smooth or rounded shapes that catch as little moving air as possible. In order to move forward, anything that wants to fly must create more thrust than the force of drag.

HOW COULD HUMANS FLY?

Without the use of flying aids, humans would have a hard time trying to fly. The main issue facing humans trying to fly is creating lift. Humans don't have large wings or light bodies compared to aircraft or flying animals. Although people can flap

DID YOU KNOW?

"Birdman rallies" are competitions of small human-powered gliders and aircraft tested by running or jumping off a pier or short bridge over water. Even though almost all designs fail, awards are given for distance and entertainment value.

their arms and push a little air around, it's not enough to lift them off the ground. People can jump, but the force of gravity on their bodies brings them back down to where they started.

One thing that is not much of a problem for humans is thrust. Humans are great runners. They have strong legs and upright bodies that let them run longer distances. However, running would only help a human while they were on the ground. With no ground to push off of, there's no way for humans to create thrust when in the air.

Another problem humans would have once in the air is dealing with drag. Human bodies have a lot of broad surface area. When humans walk or run, most of the drag hits the front of the body. This can be slightly overcome by flying with the body horizontal, like someone lying down. Many superheroes are shown flying like this.

But nothing would be holding a flying person's legs up. Anyone flying this way would get tired of holding their legs up against gravity before long. Drag would also still affect the head, shoulders, and feet.

Unless humans sprout large wings or develop psychic powers to lift themselves, they're stuck using technology to fly. Luckily, humans are very good at using technology to solve problems. Aircraft have been used by humans all over the world for more than one hundred years.

GLIDING VERSUS FLYING

If an aircraft isn't able to create enough lift to fly upward, it can still slow its fall to the ground. Paper planes and flying disc toys like Frisbee generate some lift, but still slowly fall to the ground. This is called gliding. Humans have made aircraft and suits that are very good at gliding.

Even though gliders don't make enough lift to fly, it's possible to keep one in the air for a long time. With some skill, a glider can use updrafts to gain a boost of lift. An updraft is an upward-moving current of air. Updrafts are most often created when air is heated and rises upward.

A skydiver uses a wing suit to glide.

Gliders often don't have their own source of thrust, either. Paper planes only have the thrust of the arm of the thrower. To keep moving forward, some gliders actually use gravity to help. By continuing to glide downward, gliders can gain speed. Since drag happens when an aircraft moves in any direction, the drag can be used to help the glider change direction. The falling motion turns into forward motion.

How Humans Glide

Humans have a hard time gliding on their own, but it's a bit easier than flying. Humans can glide by using hang gliders or wing suits. Hang gliders use large, broad wings to make enough lift to help them glide. Wing suits are different. They are fabric suits with flaps of cloth that connect the inside of the arm to the inside of the body, as well as the inside of the legs. By using the fabric "wings," a person in a wing suit can glide downward at high speeds. To slow down and land, users of wing suits use parachutes to create drag. Other gliders include specially designed planes with tiny engines that are only used to help take off, land, or control the plane in an emergency.

CHAPTER 3

NATURAL FLYERS

Humans might not be built to fly, but other animals are. There are thousands of species of flying creatures on Earth. Many of them fly in different and interesting ways. Other flying animals are remarkable for other reasons, such as speed or excellent hearing.

Opposite: Birds like this white-bellied sea eagle are masters at flight.

A flying fox bat, shown here, is the largest bat species.

BATS

Bats are small, flying animals that have wings made of stretched skin over a skeletal frame. Bats fly by using the leathery skin of their wings to flap and gain lift and thrust. Most bats are nocturnal. This means they're more active at night. Although many people use the phrase "blind as a bat," bats are not usually blind. Many of them have large eyes that can see well in moonlight. However, in caves and other areas with almost no light at all, bats use a special trick to find their way in the dark: echolocation. Echolocation is the ability to use the reflection, or echo, of a sound to locate things without needing to see them.

Bats are mammals, like humans. That means they give birth to live young and feed them milk until they're old enough to feed themselves. Bats are unique flyers because they're the only mammal that can actually fly on its own. There are more than one thousand species of bats living all over the world.

Bats might be the only flying mammals, but other mammals can glide. The most commonly known glider is the flying squirrel. Flying squirrels, like many glider mammals, use broad flaps of skin stretched between their limbs to glide. They do this to help them jump long distances between trees. Flying squirrels live in many parts of North America. Other gliding mammals include the sugar glider from Australia and the flying lemur from the Philippines.

This photograph shows how a flying squirrel glides to make long jumps between branches.

BIRDS

Birds are one of the most common species of flying animals on Earth. There are thousands of species of birds on the planet, and they live all over the world. Many birds migrate with the seasons in large numbers. Not all birds fly the exact same way, and some species, like penguins and ostriches, can't fly at all. Other species have special adaptations to help them survive. For example, owls can fly almost silently. This is because they have a row of feathers that stops the wind from causing their wings to make noise.

All flying birds can gain lift and thrust through flapping their wings. They do this to take off, to change direction quickly, and to fly higher.

Hummingbirds

Hummingbirds are a unique kind of bird. They're usually very small compared to other birds, but they're excellent flyers. Rather than using large wings to move lots of air at once, hummingbirds have small wings that flap very quickly. Some species of hummingbirds flap their wings as fast as eighty times per second. That kind of movement is so rapid that it's hard to hear individual wing flaps. Instead, it sounds more like a low "hum" sound. That's how hummingbirds got their name.

Hummingbirds are very strong and precise flyers and can hover in place. In order to keep those tiny wings moving so much, hummingbirds need lots of energy. They get it by using their long beaks to drink sugary nectar from flowers, much like bees. The world's smallest bird is the bee hummingbird. It weighs a little more than a paperclip.

Two white-tailed hillstar hummingbirds hover over a flower, searching for sugary nectar.

DID YOU KNOW?

The fastest bird is the peregrine falcon, which can reach speeds of 200 miles per hour (321 kmh) in a downward dive. The fastest horizontal flier is the Brazilian free-tailed bat, which has top speeds of 99 miles per hour (160 kmh).

They also have light bodies and sleek shapes to reduce drag. However, some birds have another ability: **soaring**. Birds that soar combine gliding and flying. This allows them to travel long distances while saving energy. This is a great tool for birds that spend many hours hunting other animals for food.

BUGS

Lots of insects can fly too. In fact, there are millions of flying bugs on Earth. Almost all of them use moving wings to gain lift and thrust. Bugs have an easy time flying because they're small and light. This allows them to use very small wings to carry themselves. Insects of many kinds live all over the world.

Ballooning spiders can make tangles of webs, like this. These webs can help spiders take flight.

Although they're not insects, some species of spiders have a special way of flying. They don't use wings or flaps of skin. Instead, they use their silk. First, the spider finds a place to wait for a gust of wind. Then, it releases a thin strand of silk called

DID YOU KNOW?

Some plants use rocket-like explosive power to move their seeds. The ecballium, or exploding cucumber plant, forces water into the pouch of seeds at the end of its stem. When the pressure gets high enough, the pouch breaks off and shoots seeds and water for a great distance.

gossamer. When the wind blows, the strand of silk acts like a kite or a parachute and is carried by the wind. The spider then rides along.

This trick, called **ballooning**, is mostly used by newly hatched spiders to quickly leave the nest. It does this because its many siblings will compete with it for food. The baby spiders might even begin to eat each other if they are desperate. Some adult spiders use ballooning too, but it's less common. Ballooning spiders can ride wind currents for miles before landing.

PLANTS

Spiders are not the only creatures to use wind to spread their numbers. Certain kinds of plants do this too. Dandelions are a common summer sight in many parts of the world. As the plant goes through its life cycle, it changes from a bright yellow flower to a gray ball of seeds. Each seed has a stalk with a very light collection of thin fibers. These fibers separate from the stalk when they can catch the wind or if someone blows on them. The fibers come to rest in a new spot and try to grow into a new plant.

Another plant that uses wind is the maple tree. In late summer or early autumn, maple trees drop their seeds. These seeds, called samaras, have a single wing that can help them fly in a twirling motion to try to grow a new tree. The spinning motion of the seeds resembles that of a helicopter.

A cluster of samaras hangs on a maple tree.

CHAPTER 4

FLYING AND NEW TECHNOLOGIES

Aircraft have come a long way since the original designs of the Wright brothers. With every passing year, aircraft designers improve different parts of an aircraft. Engines become more powerful. They travel faster and farther than previous aircraft. And still, new ways to use aircraft are being discovered. Future aircraft will likely be better than the ones used today.

Opposite: The space shuttle *Discovery* uses rocket boosters to launch into outer space.

The Boeing 787 Dreamliner, shown here, is one of the largest passenger planes today.

One of the most common uses for aircraft is to carry passengers over long distances. Passenger planes, or airliners, are used every day in cities all over the world. Some planes can carry more than four hundred people at one time. Planes carry people to almost any major city on Earth.

One possibility in the future of aircraft is through the use of **suborbital** flight. In suborbital flight, you fly close to outer space but do not stay in orbit like a satellite. These new aircraft would use rockets to fly extremely high up, where the air is thinner. Thinner air means less air resistance and less drag, making an aircraft able to fly faster. Less gravity also means needing less lift to stay in flight. An airliner traveling from New York City to Berlin, Germany, takes around eight hours today. A suborbital flight could make that trip in just two hours. Currently, it is difficult to make suborbital flights because these flights are expensive and can't carry a lot of passengers. With some advances in rocket technology, these flights could become much more popular.

THE SPACE RACE AND FUTURE ROCKETS

Using rockets to travel across the earth might be a new idea, but rockets have been around for centuries. Ancient rockets were more like fireworks. They couldn't carry much more weight than themselves. That changed near the end of World War II with the beginning of the space race. The space race started in the early 1950s and ended in the early 1970s. During that time, the United States and the Soviet Union were competing to create better rocket technology and explore outer space.

A company called SpaceX is attempting to pick up where the space race left off. SpaceX was started by a man named Elon Musk. He is an engineer and businessman from South Africa. SpaceX's goal is to provide a space travel service for people one day. It has become a leader in space exploration and spacecraft technology.

SpaceX CEO Elon Musk speaks at a conference in 2014.

SpaceX has gone on several important missions in the twenty-first century. For example, it was the first company to successfully reuse a rocket. In August 2017, it helped deliver supplies to the International Space Station.

Many people hope that other companies and groups will try to improve their own technology to compete with SpaceX in a new space race.

PERSONAL FLIGHT

Pilot Eric Scott shows how to use a jet pack at an event in England in August 2007.

Flying in planes and helicopters is helpful, but it doesn't come close to feeling like a superhero flying through the air. Humans may not be able to fly without help, but technology might make flying like a superhero more possible.

It takes something like a personal aircraft to recreate the feeling of flying like a superhero. **Jet packs** are a popular example of a personal aircraft. Not only are they common in science-fiction stories and

DID YOU KNOW?

Some aircraft can go from flying like planes to flying like helicopters. One example of this is the V-22 Osprey. It can rotate its engines and either use them like forward-facing propellers or downward-facing rotors.

movies, but real ones do exist. They do have their limits, though. Current working jet packs are heavy. They have to carry the fuel to fly and have some way to make lift and thrust. They also need people to have special training to use safely. Most working jet packs keep the user in an upright position, similar to standing or sitting. Few jet packs use wings. They can't fly forward very fast. Flying like a superhero, arms outstretched and lying flat, is difficult for most people and uncomfortable after a while.

HOVERCRAFT

It might be possible to recreate the sensation of flying without as much risk as a jet pack. **Hovercraft** are another popular idea from science-fiction stories, movies, and comics.

Hovercraft are vehicles made to hover, or float, above the ground. While not able to fly up as high, hovercraft still deal with lift, drag, gravity, and thrust. Currently, not many working types of hovercraft exist.

The Hydropump Jet Pack

There is one kind of jet pack that people can try for fun without much special training. It's called a hydropump jet pack, and there are companies that make and rent them to customers. This kind of jet pack is flown over water. It uses a powerful water pump to draw water in through a big hose. The water is then shot out the bottom of the pack. The stream of water lifts the rider into the air. Some versions of this look like a backpack. Others are more like a skateboard. The device can fly only as high as the hose is long. Flying over water is also a little safer. If someone crashes, they fall into the water and are less likely to get hurt. There are also usually experts nearby to help in case of an emergency.

A hovercraft moves over water quickly.

So far, the most common type of hovercraft is the Air Cushion Vehicle, or the ACV. The ACV uses powerful air blowers to fill a balloon-like pouch underneath it. The pouch catches the air and only lets the air go downward. This lifts the craft and lets it float over water and land. The ACV then uses a large fan and fins to move forward and steer.

One possible way humans might have hovercraft in the future is through magnetic tracks. Some fast-moving passenger trains today use powerful magnets to float just above their tracks. However, the trains still require the tracks to remain hovering.

GLOSSARY

AIRCRAFT Machines that can fly, like planes and helicopters.

BALLOONING The way spiders use the wind and their silk to travel great distances in the air.

DRAG The effect of air resistance on an object moving in any direction.

FORCE A physical expression of energy that can move things.

GLIDE An action similar to flight but without enough lift to sustain flying.

GOSSAMER Thin strands of light silk that some spiders use to ride wind currents.

GRAVITY The downward force that pulls all things toward the center of the earth.

HOVERCRAFT A vehicle designed to float and move just above the surface of the earth.

JET PACK A personal aircraft that resembles a backpack.

LIFT The upward force generated by wings or rotors on aircraft and animals.

MYTH Ancient stories told by different cultures.

SOARING A combination of gliding and flying that some birds use to travel long distances.

SPACE RACE A period from the 1950s to 1970s when the United States and USSR competed to explore outer space and improve rocket technology.

SUBORBITAL A method of travel that is close to outer space but not high enough to orbit the earth.

THRUST The force that aircraft and flying creatures use to fly forward.

FIND OUT MORE

BOOKS

Buckley, James Jr. *Who Were the Wright Brothers?*
New York: Grosset & Dunlap, 2015.

Nahum, Andrew. *Flight*. New York: DK Publishing,
2011.

Newquist, HP. *From Here to There: The Story of
How We Transport Ourselves and Everything Else*.
New York: Viking, 2017.

Wilgus, Alison. *Flying Machines: How the Wright
Brothers Soared*. Science Comics. New York:
First Second, 2017.

WEBSITES

11 of the World's Most Famous Warplanes

https://www.britannica.com/list/11-of-the-worlds-most-famous-warplanes

This list goes over several of history's most famous aircraft. Each one is shown with a picture, description, and interesting facts.

The History and Future of Blimp Technology

http://www.npr.org/templates/story/story.php?storyId=127932754

Blimps aren't the most common way to fly, but they have definitely earned a place in history. This interview specifically examines the history of blimps and other airships.

NASA: Air Transportation in the 21st Century

https://www.nasa.gov/centers/langley/news/factsheets/FutofFlt.html

This article in NASA's archive covers improvements to the industry of flight in the last one hundred years, including safety measures and aircraft designs.

INDEX

Page numbers in **boldface** are illustrations. Entries in **boldface** are glossary terms.

ABOUT THE AUTHOR

JORDAN JOHNSON is a writer and science enthusiast from Wisconsin. He has studied aviation and the history of aircraft since he was a teenager. He enjoys playing flight simulator games and testing his own crazy aircraft designs in different computer programs. He enjoys reading new articles about aviation and aerospace technology.